The Birds Were the Only Ones Singing

The Birds Were the Only Ones Singing

Matt Dolezal

Copyright © 2024 Matt Dolezal

The moral right of the author has been asserted.

Apart from any fair dealing for the purposes of research or private study, or criticism or review, as permitted under the Copyright, Designs and Patents Act 1988, this publication may only be reproduced, stored or transmitted, in any form or by any means, with the prior permission in writing of the publishers, or in the case of reprographic reproduction in accordance with the terms of licences issued by the Copyright Licensing Agency. Enquiries concerning reproduction outside those terms should be sent to the publishers.

This is a work of fiction. Names, characters, businesses, places, events and incidents are either the products of the author's imagination or used in a fictitious manner. Any resemblance to actual persons, living or dead, or actual events is purely coincidental.

Troubador Publishing Ltd
Unit E2 Airfield Business Park
Harrison Road, Market Harborough
Leicestershire LE16 7UL
Tel: 0116 279 2299
Email: books@troubador.co.uk
Web: www.troubador.co.uk

ISBN 978 1 80514 499 1

British Library Cataloguing in Publication Data.
A catalogue record for this book is available from the British Library.

Printed and bound in Great Britain by 4edge Limited
Typeset in 11pt Minion Pro by Troubador Publishing Ltd, Leicester, UK

For my Wife, Friends and Family and all those passing ships I have met on the way.

Contents

1 NATURE
A Place of Tranquillity	3
My Garden Mate the Robin	4
The Ocean	5
The Greedy Snake	6

2 COMMUNITY
Market Town	13
In Our Name	14
The Birds Were the Only Ones Singing	15
The Matchbox Man	17

3 FOLK
Unsettled Status	21
The Hustler	22
News from Nowhere (Inspired by William Morris)	23
The Luddites' Lament	25

4 LOVE
Aberystwyth	29
Rush Hour Crush	30
Truth and Love	31
Is There Anything Left to Say about Love?	34

5 LOSS
The Wild Pear of Cubbington   39
Technological Wasteland   42
The Birds Stopped Singing   43
When the Landscape Shifts   44

6 METAMORPHOSIS
Cords of Life   47

1
Nature

A Place of Tranquillity

There is a place in my heart,
Away from all the noise of the crowd;
There is a place tucked away,
Along the backwaters of the River Dart.

Escape the busy cities and towns,
Down ancient tracks and trails,
Follow red-tailed bumble bees and meadow browns,
Watch them frequent foxgloves and red campion,
Among the bracken and the fern,
Here they will prevail.

Along an ancient wall,
Fleabane and navelwort,
Will grow tall.

Drop down to Bow Bridge,
You will find a quiet creek,
Sit by The Waterman,
Amongst the oak and ash,
You may see a kingfisher flash.

My Garden Mate the Robin

As I work around the garden,
I am observed.

While the blackbird may fly in,
Just to see what worms I may unearth,
It is the robin who comes in,
Just to give his two pennies' worth.

While I snip, grapple and weed,
The robin he'll perch next to me,
And natter in my ear,
While occasionally swooping in for an insect to feed!
However, what he talks about,
I have absolutely no idea!

The Ocean

I am drawn to the ocean;
It awakens my senses,
Which stirs my emotions.

In the city I feel tense,
But here I relax my defence;
This enables me to embrace all that is real,
So that I am able to feel,
Gaia, the essence, the embodiment,
The geneses of all that is life.

Every sound,
From a trickle to a roar,
The motion of every wave,
As the tide hits the shore.
As it crashes against the rocks,
Through the channels,
It then trickles and it pours,
The foam, the spray,
That I feel on my face,
The sting of the salt,
That quickly goes away.
The light that reflects
The different colours,
As if they were painted specks.

It was here when life first began,
Long before,
Every woman and every man.

The Greedy Snake

In the woods down by the lake,
There lived a very greedy snake.
Anything that moved,
Which caught his eye,
He would most definitely take.

One time, in his youth,
He saw two young rats,
He was eager to pursue,
For this he could not wait.
The leanest and the fittest of the rats,
He got away,
Leaving his brother to meet his fate.

As time went on,
The only animals that were left in the woods,
The snake found to be
Too fast, too agile, too big, they had wings,
Or they were just too smart,
To feed the snake's insatiable heart.

Then one day the snake spied that second rat,
Remember the one that got away!
By now the snake knew
That he could not catch that rat;
By now the snake was too old and fat.
But in his old age, the snake had grown crafty,

For he could use this rat in another way;
For the snake, this could pay.

So, the snake beckoned over to the rat,
He tried to get his attention,
But the rat was wary,
For he remembered;
He suspected a trap.

"I know you; it was you who snuffed my brother,"
Said the rat.
"Oh, it was not me; it was another,"
Replied the snake. The rat paused for thought;
He then did retort,
"Are you sure?"
Then he reflected
"Well, it was some time ago, I guess;
My head's a bloomin' mess."

"I can protect you," said the snake.
"Why don't you come down with me to the lake.
I know your fears,
They are the same as mine,
But together we'll be fine."

Down by the lake,
A plan was hatched,
Between the rat and the snake:

The snake persuaded the rat,
Of threats from outside and above.

"It is the birds,
For which I am most perturbed.
They swoop and soar.
No, it is not I,
Whom you should fear;
They can peck out your eye!
They will take your young,
And they will do it just for fun!

"The way we must beat them,
Is that we must meet them,
Play them at their own game.
Go into the nests when they are away,
Take their eggs and young just the same.
But bring me the spoils,
And we can share them out.
I'm getting hungry, so don't hang about!"

Well, after this, the rat was fired up,
So, he went out and did as the snake had asked:
He decimated every nest to the last.

In a short space of time,
There were no more eggs, or chicks, left in the woods.
"Bring me more," said the snake.
"But there aren't no more left to have; I have done all I can,"
Was the rat's response.

Annoyed and disappointed the plan had gone wrong,
The snake turned on the rat and said,
"Prepare to sing your last song.

"If that is all you can do,
Then, my furry friend, I will have to eat you!"
The rat was trapped and cornered,
And then he was gone.
Now all alone,
The snake had eaten the rat,
To the last bone.

So, the wood now seemed to feel like
A very empty place:
No more animals, not even a snail.
The snake then looked behind him,
And noticed his tail.
"Hello," he said,
"I wonder what you taste like…"
He took a bite and then went quite pale,
Then took one more,
And that's the end of the tale.

2
Community

Market Town

These ancient towns and villages,
Built of local stone,
Here for millennia,
Communities have grown.

From farmer's field to dinner fork,
Via butcher, to baker, to cheesemaker,
It is just a short walk
Back to your home.

All about these ancient towns,
Long-standing trades,
Have been passed down.

Community is strong,
When friendships are forged.
Trust is a must,
So, we must not let these towns rust;
We must not let them vanish into dust!

In Our Name

In our name a king is crowned;
A nation is born;
The people are fed.

In our name, seeds are sown to the ground;
The land is torn;
The old king is dead.

In our name, the ground is torn,
Torn from the people who work the land,
To make way for the new king's nation,
The new king's orders;
All protests have been banned.

While we carry on our lives,
We kindly avert our eyes,
To the massacres that are carried out in our name.

We hide our shame;
We divert the blame,
At those who pose a threat to our ill-begotten gain.

The Birds Were the Only Ones Singing

It was a silent spring;
The birds were the only ones singing.
There were no festivals that year,
And it felt like there was no chance,
Of winning.

All the planes had ceased flying;
The birds had the skies to themselves;
The shops were all empty,
Because people had been panic buying.

The animals had reclaimed the streets,
People had left them behind;
They had retreated into their homes.
No one was going anywhere,
Ever grateful for their telephones.

As we all watched the news with bated breath,
The virus swept through our communities.
In their thousands people were dying:
Many key workers, doctors and nurses,
Paramedics, bus drivers, teachers, binmen, shopworkers,
And the vulnerable,
All lost their lives.
Yet so many saw it as a hoax,

And were in denial,
For a moment the world paused.
All the plans had ceased.
A time of reflection,
A society correction,
Not knowing its direction.
People looked to the politicians,
In the hope that they would offer
at least some attrition.

The politicians just ducked and dived;
They told so many lies.
They weaved their webs of confusion,
Which led to the allusion of hypocrisy,
The erosion of our democracy.

The illusion,
Of a government in control,
Was brought into question,
Until hope and inspiration, anticipation,
Of a vaccination.

We learnt new skills in isolation,
While some made bread;
Others gave education.

But thankful we all are for those key workers,
The doctors and nurses,
Paramedics, bus drivers, teachers, binmen,
and shopworkers.

The Matchbox Man

The Matchbox Man will come today;
Go tell the others, he's on his way.
A familiar face,
From a distant place,
Somewhere we once called home.

Matchboxes are ubiquitous and cheap;
However, these ones are significant and unique:
They carry a connection of somewhere,
We once called home.

They display images and messages,
Of a communist ideal,
A way of life,
That hides what is real,
But hidden inside are secret letters,
From loved ones,
Which tell us how "they feel".
This is how we bypass the tapped phones,
With secret messages,
From a place we once called home.

3
Folk

Unsettled Status

I may not have been born here,
But for as long as I can remember,
This has been my home.
Embedded within this community,
They treat me as their own.

Lifelong friends I have made,
To society I have paid.
Through my work and activity,
Together we are a community.

United in spirit,
Despite our diversity,
Together we are one.

However, there are those,
Who do not understand;
They seek to divide us;
They tell us their thoughts;
They say I don't belong;
They say I must be gone.
Made to leave my home,
To forever roam,
All alone in a land,
That's not my own.

The Hustler

The excuses we make,
That parallel the actions we take,
I often hear,
"If I don't do it, someone else will."

The deals we do and the people we screw,
What we make on the side here and there,
In the back pocket goes, whatever is spare.

Just turn a blind eye,
And don't ask why;
Just smile as you lie,
Don't be shy.

"If I don't do it, someone else will."

The consequential actions,
Of the activities we speak,
Are beneficial to the ruthless,
But crush the meek.

There will come a time in your hour of need,
When the people whom you have screwed and crushed,
Will simply walk away,
And watch you bleed.

News from Nowhere

(Inspired by William Morris)

I awoke in my home;
However, all was not the same.
When I ventured out, the people whom I met
Had no concept of profit and gain.
Gone were all the glass towers
And symbols of imperialist powers.

A new world I have found
Right here at my door.
I must go out and seek others;
I must find out more.

As I travelled out along the upper Thames reaches,
I found a way of life
That was simple and pure.
with a people who were happy.
They were without greed,
or the fear of war.

I celebrated these days,
The end of capitalism,
Said goodbye to the monetary prison,
Said goodbye to globalism.

I welcomed a new-found localism,
Where people work alongside their friends and neighbours,
In communal collectivism.

The ambitions of wealth and Westminster
Are confined to the history books.
People are free, to get on with a life
Of independent libertarianism.

Alas I awoke once more;
It was all a Utopian dream.
A dream that can inspire,
A dream to awaken my inner fire!
We can, we must, strive for peace and equality,
A time to end all poverty. An end to a system,
In which people and planet are slaves
To the economy,
Replaced with a system
In which people and planet have autonomy.

The Luddites' Lament

In the jobs that I have found,
A living I can take,
But this life I am bound,
With what I can make.

The machines are taking over
The jobs that exist;
Soon they'll take mine,
But I will try to resist.

My work may be toil,
It may be tough,
But it puts food on the table,
And stops me sleeping rough.

My art is my escape,
A chance to create;
It gives me hope,
Hope that I could have a better life,
If someone thinks it's great.

But now, alas, the machines
Do "art".
They will paint you a picture,
Write you a song;
They'll even replicate poetry.
But the tin man has no heart;
To me this just feels wrong.

Art comes from real-life experience;
It comes from the soul.
A machine may replicate a style,
But it will never be real or whole.

4
Love

Aberystwyth

The sun is shining and
The sky is blue,
While I am stuck in the bathroom,
Clinging to the loo.
Regretting the night, I spent
With you.
It wasn't the company
That was so wrong,
More so all the beer,
And ending the night,
With a bong.
Patchy memories
Are recalled, of a fight
With a giant banana,
And King Kong.
Students running into the sea,
And me desperately looking for a back ally,
To have a pee.
A dodgy kebab, and pissed-up girls,
With short skirts, with slurry words,
And I with blurry eyes.
One, she offers me some of her fries.
We joke and tell each other lies,
Which we know cannot be true.
But it's all good fun,
And she is there,
When I am woken by the sun.

Rush Hour Crush

Every morning on the 8:15,
From Dollis Hill,
I see my rush-hour crush,
I think her name might be Jill,
I really think she's lush.

Each morning, our eyes
Do meet,
And we exchange a smile.
I save her a seat;
I have been wanting to ask her out,
For a while,
But I am such a wuss.

I might submit to the *Metro*,
That she caught my eye,
And if she does reply,
At least then I'll know,
If I am her rush-hour crush.

Truth and Love

In a time when no one dared,
To speak the truth,
A time when people lived,
In contempt of one another,
There lived a widow,
By the name of Ruth,
Who lived with her late husband's
Mother.

People did ask her why
She cared for her mother-in-law.
"For you are not related;
You could just walk out the door."

To which she replied,
"If I did not, who else would?
I do so through love and compassion;
It's my duty and loyalty,
To my late husband;
It was his dying will."

Ruth could not understand,
Why so many people,
Across the land,
Did not think as she.

All around her, she did see,
A society, that was unequal,
Full of extravagant excess.
People who seemed possessed, obsessed,
By their own self desires.
Yet so many were left dispossessed.

Ruth thought about those who were forgotten,
Those who were ignored,
Weakened through illness and misfortune,
They had slipped through the net,
All they had left went to pay their debts.

So again, after reflection of what she saw, Ruth spoke out,
"So, what of the poor,
What of the weak,
Those who are struggling,
All those who are meek?"

"Could not one of you give up your time,
As I have, to help them out?"

Then a voice did shout;
The voice did speak,
"Don't be so woke!"

Ruth turned to look that person in the eye,
And she spoke,
"Woke? What is it to be woke?
To be awake?
To be socially aware?
To speak the truth!
To be opposite is to be ignorant,
And to not care."

Is There Anything Left to Say about Love?

Is there anything left to say about love,
Which hasn't been said before,
Without sounding like a bore?

What I do know is,
When it strikes,
It can knock you to the floor,
But leave you
Wanting more.

We can follow those we adore,
Like sheep,
But they may tease,
Or even appease you,
Just to try and please you,
But they will string you along,
While all along,
They just think you're a geek.

They may even sleep with you,
Just because they know you're an easy lay,
But this kind of love,
You must stay away;
It will only do you wrong;
It will drive you insane!

Real love comes,
When you find that someone,
That unique person you may meet,
In the Kazbar,
Or sat next to you on the train.

You don't stop talking,
From Euston to Dunblane.
You find you share the same passions,
Love of life,
Follow the same band,
And love to travel;
Of course, you don't agree on everything,
But you take these differences in hand.
But it's that connection,
That spark,
You both understand.
Then you realise,
You've missed your station;
You've gone beyond your destination.

Do you leave them on the train and say goodbye?
This may be the last time you see them,
You cannot deny.

As you leave the train,
You exchange details, in vain.
A hope this brief encounter,
Doesn't remain,
On the train.

5
Loss

The Wild Pear of Cubbington

In a time when it seemed,
The whole world,
Was at war,
For four long years,
Or more.
The old king died,
And King George III
was crowned.

Away from all the noise
Of the crowd,
There is a quiet corner
Of Warwickshire to be found.
As the River Leam does flow,
It winds its way through Cubbington woods,
Where a young pear sapling begins to grow.

Unnoticed at first in those early years,
Shielded and protected by
Brambles and briars,
From browsing rabbits and deer,
Nurtured and entangled,
Into the ancient woods'
Web of life.
The tree grew strong,
And blossomed;
It became resistant to ecological strife.

As kings and queens,
Did come and go,
Our pear tree continued to grow,
Providing food and shelter,
For all the wildlife it came to know.

Many summers and winters did pass,
While every few years the pear
Would generate a mast.
A bumper crop for all who came,
A chance for offspring to get ahead of the game.

Untouched through the centuries, this cycle of life,
In the spring, lovers would come to admire the blossom,
then make hay,
As in autumn, fungus and worm would help the leaves to decay.

Then, in 1940, war came close by,
As Nazi Luftwaffe did fill the sky!
In the woods two bombs did land,
A close encounter with man's,
Destructive hand.

Yes, our tree did survive,
But it was Coventry,
Which took the harshest blow.
As so many lost their lives,
The distant fires
Made the night sky glow.

While this new war did rage on,
A young Czech soldier and his *miláčku*,
Would come to pick mushrooms,
While having some fun.

Years later, their children
Would come to play in the woods;
Sometimes they would be Peter Pan,
While other times they would be Robin Hood.
The children grew up, then moved away.
One did return; his ashes now stay.

Now a mature tree,
And well known,
The people of Cubbington
Claim this tree in their hearts as their own.
The second largest wild pear in all of England,
A local landmark it became,
Voted tree of the year,
This brought fame.

Then five years did pass;
It was declared, "These ancient woods will have to go!
We want a high-speed train,"
The Government decreed.
Devastated and shocked, the locals said, "No!"
But for the profiteers there was too much to gain,
Driven by profit and greed.
Now our pear is gone, as are the ancient Cubbington woods.
But in memories and cuttings,
Our wild pear will live on.

Technological Wasteland

We once called these places our homes;
Now all I see are warehouses,
Filled with drones.
There were once fields and woodlands,
Where folk would work the land;
There were once workshops,
Where craftsman made things by hand.

Gone now are the people,
Who called this place
their own,
replaced by robots who toil alone.

Robots don't ask questions;
They don't need to be paid.
The once proud craftsman,
Swept aside,
They have lost their trade.

Robots are efficient,
They work so fast,
All expectations have been surpassed.

But there is one problem
The zeitgeist overlooked in haste:
If no one ever gets paid,
Then there is no one to buy what has been made,
So, what is produced,
Becomes a mountain of technological waste.

The Birds Stopped Singing

They are late!
Why, what, who?
The house martins of course!
I am worried;
Have they met an awful fate?

*Maybe they have been
Blown off course?
So how late are they?*
Well, it is the end of May;
They should have arrived by April,
That's what they say.

June, July pass by,
Still no house martins in the sky.
Similarly, the swallows and swifts,
Also seem to be adrift.

As August arrives,
Something for sure is not right.
There are no birds in flight.

No chattering in the trees;
The dawn chorus is muted;
The avian fate is disputed…

A likely clue,
Points to flu…

When the Landscape Shifts

A huge change has come.
In life we experience so many changes.
But this cannot be undone.

There are certain things,
That seem more certain than others.
A continuous thread,
Our daily bread,
There when we need them,
Our family, our friends, our lovers.

They may have always been around,
Or suddenly appear in our lives,
To whisk our feet right off the ground.

But even mountains will grow,
They will erode;
Rivers may change their course,
Continents even shift;
It is nature's dynamic force.

Although we may not notice these changes,
As we do the seasons,
There is one obvious reason,
When that change comes, it is at an adaptable pace,
It is the sudden loss, which is hard to face.

6
Metamorphosis

Cords of Life

I hear a rustle of leaves.
I feel the sun on my face.
I open my eyes;
I notice a gentle breeze.
As the sun beams filter,
Through the forest canopy,
The light dances on the ground,
With such elegant grace.

A robin flies in,
He perches close by,
He looks me in the eye;
He is certainly not shy.
I drift away;
He disappears from sight,
He has no time to stay.

The light is fading.
In the distance,
I hear a sole bird sing.
I close my eyes,
As I sink into the ground;
Not a human sound,
Is to be found.

Every cell in my body,
Becomes absorbed,
Into the endless, mycelium cord.
Through this network I do travel,
At great speed on a psychedelic tour,
Meandering beneath the forest floor.

Sugars and electric currents
Pass me by;
I am everywhere at once,
Don't ask me how or why.

Sucked up by the roots
Of the wild pear,
The oak and the ash,
I become at one with the forest,
In one enlightened flash.
An alternate consciousness,
I am now aware,
I am no longer myself;
I have no eyes, no ears,
But I sense light and dark,
Cold and warmth;
Gone now are all my anxieties and fears.